True Escape
and Survival Stories

True Escape and Survival Stories

by Gurney Williams III

Illustrated by Michael Deas

Franklin Watts   New York   London   1977

Library of Congress Cataloging in Publication Data

Williams, Gurney, 1941-
  True escape and survival stories.

  Includes index.
  1. Biography—20th century—Juvenile literature.
2. Heroes—Biography—Juvenile literature. 3. Adventure and adventurers—Biography—Juvenile literature.
4. Escapes—Juvenile literature. I. Title.
CT120.W55   910'.453 [B]   77–1421
ISBN 0–531–00119–9

Contents

True Escape and Survival Stories

Chapter 1

A fuel tank blows up and cripples a spaceship on the way to the moon . . .

Lightning pins a mountain climber to a rock . . .

An innocent prisoner faces a cruel guard who has the power to order death sentences by pointing his finger . . .

And then the question is survival. Who lives through these crises and disasters? There are some surprising answers in these true stories.

Most people think that only the strong survive. But this belief is not always true. Survivors are often physically weak, timid, and scared. They cry. Frequently, they don't know what to do. They can't control their lives like supermen or bionic women. They're not much different from people you know. From *you*.

Myth has it that survivors are lone heroes and heroines, boldly independent. Surprise again: sometimes the only

people who make it home alive are the ones who admit they
need other people. Like young and homesick children, survivors sometimes grasp at thoughts of home. What they
think and feel keeps death at bay as surely as the meager
rations they eat or drink.

Survival often depends on luck. Where were you sitting
on the plane when it crashed? Where were you standing
when lightning hit the mountain? But these accounts show
there's more to survival than luck or physical strength or
steely independence.

For instance, here's a story about a real person in a nightmare world, a starving man who had to depend on his good
dreams to save him. His name was Viktor Frankl. He was
a prisoner of the Germans during the Second World War.

The scene was a concentration camp, a prison. It was
called Auschwitz, and it was located in the southeast corner
of Poland. From the outside, Auschwitz looked innocent
enough. There was room for 200,000 prisoners, housed in
solid brick structures. The camp had tree-lined streets. Its
front gate was marked with an encouraging sign: "WORK
BRINGS FREEDOM."

But inside the walls of barbed wire, Auschwitz was or-
ganized to kill masses of people. It was the keystone of a
plan by the Nazi leaders of Germany to kill as many Jews
as possible. Somewhere between 600,000 and 1,000,000 men,
women, and children died here at Auschwitz. The odds of
survival were poor—maybe one in ten. Inside the camp,
Germans herded thousands of people at a time into large
rooms, and turned on jets of poisonous gas. Then they
burned the bodies, and piled them into mass graves. They

made separate piles for belongings—eyeglasses and shoes, for instance—shed by victims just before their death.

Some survived Auschwitz. The American journalist Edward R. Murrow reported on the survivors the rescuers found when they invaded the death camp. He said the survivors applauded those who had come to set them free. But they were so weak, they sounded like babies clapping.

All during the war, death howled up and down the military rows of the Auschwitz barracks. It destroyed almost everyone. What shielded those who survived? Luck was partly responsible. Good health was important too. The strong were better able to fight off disease. But there was more, several of the survivors wrote later. Those who made it clung to the idea that there was a reason to go on living. The survivors wrote that once a prisoner gave up trying to stay alive, he or she was doomed. Life went out of their eyes and their bodies were prey to fatal illness.

Those who stayed alive tried to help others stay alive, too. The small group of prisoners who tried to survive by helping the Nazis—some inmates even aided in the executions—died sooner. German soldiers used them for a while, then killed them, too.

Those who survived clung to important values. They respected life and rejected the law of the jungle that says only the strong survive.

None of this, of course, guaranteed life. There is no simple moral here. Many good, religious people died. The trains arrived frequently, packed eighty people to a car. The people spilled out on the railroad siding when the huge doors of the cars opened. They walked, sometimes hopefully, under the gate with the welcoming sign overhead. Most didn't survive inside the camp.

Viktor Frankl's train arrived one cold dawn. Guards in watchtowers looked down on the ragged group as they shuffled toward the barbed wire fences.

Women in one line, men in another, the prisoners were swallowed one by one into the life and death of the camp.

The tired, grimy men moved slowly toward a German officer. As Frankl walked closer, he could see that the officer was tall, wearing a fresh Nazi uniform. He looked relaxed. His left arm reached across his stomach and held up his right elbow so that his right hand was raised near his chin. As each prisoner came to him, the officer pointed with his right hand, to the right or to the left. Prisoners were told to go where he pointed.

Right. Left. Left. Left. Left. Right. Frankl could see most prisoners were being sent to the left. What did that mean?

It was Frankl's turn. The officer hesitated. He put both hands on Frankl's shoulders. He turned him slowly to the right and pushed him on.

It wasn't until later in the day when Frankl found out what it meant to be sent to the left. Those who followed the officer's point were led into a large building with the word "bath" written over the doors. Each got a piece of soap. But the soap was a trick to make them move inside without panic. There were no baths inside. When the doors were closed, poisonous gas filled the building and killed them all. Frankl had been saved by the lazy whim of a German officer.

Most of the arriving prisoners hadn't been so lucky.

Frankl estimated that more than a thousand men and women were sent to their deaths that day by a pointing officer in a spotless uniform.

The other prisoners fell into a painful, numbing routine. It was easy to give up hope at Auschwitz. Prisoners slept on shelves about seven feet wide, nine men and two blankets to a shelf. Three blasts of a whistle woke them before dawn. They forced swollen feet into wet shoes and marched to work through snowy fields. When shoes wore out, they walked barefoot in the snow.

Frankl's job was laying railroad tracks. This was rugged work. It became almost impossible to do because of the lack of food. A small piece of bread and a little broth was the daily ration. Days seemed longer than weeks.

One of Frankl's friends in the camp had a dream one night about freedom. A voice in his dream told the man, a composer of music, that he would be told anything he wanted to know. The prisoner had just one question: When will the war be over for me?

The mysterious voice in the dream told him: "March thirtieth, 1945." It was only about a month away.

The man awoke happy, and his fresh hopes carried him through the early days of March. Then bad news about the war began filtering into the camp. The Germans were holding out. The war was dragging on. Rescuers—the armies marching against Germany—were still far away. On March 29, the man suddenly ran a high fever. He lost consciousness the next day. And he died on March 31, the day after the deadline in his dream of freedom. The dream had not lied; the war was over for him.

Frankl said there were many other deaths whose real cause was loss of hope. For instance, the death rate in the camp soared during the week after Christmas in 1944. The reason, Frankl is certain, is that many prisoners had harbored faith that they would be home for Christmas. When their faith was broken, their bodies grew weaker and diseases like typhus were able to kill them.

Frankl himself clung to thoughts of his wife. She was a prisoner, too, but he didn't know where. He had no way of knowing that he would never see her again. She died a prisoner.

One cold morning, working in a trench, he carried on an imaginary conversation with her in his mind. Is there some reason to go on living? he asked.

It was almost as if someone were calling him.

"*Yes,*" said a voice in his mind. And in that instant, he saw a light go on in a farmhouse far away. He kept working, drawing strength from his love for his wife, until he was sure she was nearby. His warming feeling grew until suddenly he felt as if he could reach out and touch her hand. A bird flew down in front of him and landed on the dirt he had dug from the ditch. The bird stared at him, unafraid.

Hope kept Frankl alive until the war was almost over, when he had been moved to another camp. Then hope alone wasn't enough.

The Germans were retreating daily. Many of the prisoners were moved to other camps farther from the changing battle lines. Most of those left in Frankl's camp were feverish and delirious, although Frankl himself was still able to do a little work.

Then one day it appeared that the nightmare was over.

The gates were thrown open. An aluminum-colored car with red crosses painted on its side drove into the camp. The car was from the International Red Cross. It carried medicine and cigarettes and good news: the Germans had yielded the camp to the Red Cross. The people in the car took pictures of smiling prisoners. Then the car left for a nearby farm. They said it was temporary Red Cross headquarters. The sun set. For the prisoners this was their first good day in years.

That night, German officers arrived in the camp with trucks. They told the prisoners to climb on board. They were being taken to a camp where they were to be traded for German prisoners. Everyone would be free within two days, the officers said.

Frankl waited near the back of the group of prisoners. The group dwindled as the trucks left. Thirteen prisoners climbed on what was supposed to be the second-to-last truck, and it rumbled away. There were no other trucks in sight.

Frankl and a handful of prisoners had been left behind.

A strong and cruel person might have pushed his way aboard the last truck to leave. Instead, Frankl merely grumbled and waited, and waited some more. Finally, he and the others lay down in one of the camp's small houses. They fell asleep expecting a truck to arrive any minute to take them to freedom. Hours passed.

The other prisoners, meanwhile, bounced in the backs of their trucks to another camp nearby. They climbed off. Expecting to be released soon, they entered the camp's huts. And then the soldiers locked them in and set fire to the huts. All of those prisoners died.

Frankl awoke late that night when rifles began crackling

outside his camp. Flashes from the shooting lit up the walls of the house. Cannons rumbled. In the first seconds of light and noise, the man in the bunk above Frankl's jumped in panic, shoes first, onto Frankl's stomach. Frankl leapt out of bed and dropped to the floor, trying to hide in shadows below the dancing light of the gunfire.

Frankl realized what was happening. The battle line had come to the prison. The Germans hadn't surrendered after all. Now they were fighting to hold on to the camp.

The battle lasted until dawn. When the sun came up, it shone on a white surrender flag over the camp. Frankl was free.

Chapter 2

Quinton Stockwell Gives Up

Quinton Stockwell's bad luck really began in 1676 when a band of Indians set fire to his house. Months later he still hadn't found the time to repair the place. And now, in September of 1677, the days were getting colder. He was probably wondering how he would get through the winter.

Months later, Stockwell wrote down what happened to him the night of September 19. He recorded almost everything, even when he made mistakes. His writing shows that even though he was timid, he had the courage to face himself as he was.

The sun had just set, but it wasn't yet dark that evening when the Indians attacked. They rushed into town shouting and firing guns at the English settlers. By chance, Stockwell was carrying a pistol when he heard the noise. But it wasn't loaded. He had no choice, he thought, but to run.

He hoped to hide in a swamp. But the Indians never let

him out of their sight. Again and again they shot at him, gaining ground until one was only about fifty feet away. Stockwell splashed into the waters and deep mud of the swamp. In a few seconds he found it impossible to go on. He slipped and fell. Instantly an Indian was by his side, his hatchet high over Stockwell's head.

Stockwell drew his unloaded gun and pointed it at the Indian. Both of the men must have been covered with mud.

The Indian brave demanded the gun. He said Stockwell wouldn't be hurt if he gave up.

Stockwell refused.

The brave told Stockwell he didn't have a chance. Other Indians had burned the town and killed many of its people. Give up, he told Stockwell. He said surrender was the only way to stay alive.

He was lying. The town had not been destroyed. But Stockwell was likely to believe what he was told. Then, his clothes soaked and filthy, he walked back with the Indians to his house.

Maybe he could still get away, he thought. The first chance came when they put him up on a horse. He thought of kicking the horse in the side, making it bolt away. But the hope faded when the horse began to walk. It was slow and old. It walked as if it wanted to go to sleep.

Maybe there was another way, he thought. The Indians told him to round up all his horses for them. He said he would. He began plotting again. If he could just jump on one of his own animals he could ride away like a shot. He called to his horses. But the Indians, watching, scared the animals. Quinton Stockwell couldn't get near his own horses. The Indians said it was time to go.

So they tied Quinton Stockwell up on the back of a slow horse and led him away from his house, north toward cold mountains. The Indians had killed many—though not all— of the people in his town. They had taken many others prisoner. He didn't know whether he would ever come back.

Still close to home, he was a slave of wandering tribesmen. They probably didn't know themselves where they were going, or what they would do with him. It was dark now, and his town disappeared quickly behind him.

They rode all night. The next morning the Indians stopped to rest for a couple of hours and began marking notches in trees. Some of the bold notches stood for Englishmen they had killed in Quinton Stockwell's town. Others stood for captives. In the middle of making the notches, the Indians began to argue over Stockwell.

Three of them were fighting to be Quinton Stockwell's master. Each said he had captured the white man. Each said he deserved Stockwell as a slave. Stockwell was sure he was about to die. He knew his death was one way to end the argument. Suddenly the three Indians turned to him. They asked him to settle the fight by saying who his master was. Stockwell didn't want to take sides. He was too frightened to choose.

The Indians shouted at him to answer. The whole camp was watching Stockwell.

Three braves had captured him, he said. He had three masters, he told them.

It turned out to be a wise thing to say.

The Indians decided to share him. The fight was over. Stockwell even got a little food from his three captors.

The march lasted all day. At night, the Indians tied Stockwell's arms and legs to stakes so he couldn't move. He was so tired he never noticed the stakes. At daybreak they rode on again, zigzagging around trees, aiming for the cold north country.

They had gotten as far as what is today Northfield, Massachusetts, when Stockwell found out why they had traveled so hard. His hopes rose again. It was probably an Indian scout who brought the news: English soldiers were following them. Rescuers were on the way.

In minutes the Indians broke camp. They called in their hunters and slung weapons over their backs. They divided into several small groups and struck out in different directions, planning to come together somewhere else. They crossed rivers, and crossed them back again. They signaled by hooting like owls and howling like wolves.

The English never had a chance of finding them. In a short time the Indians had left the rescuers thirty miles behind. Stockwell's masters were so far ahead, they decided to stop and have a party. The English, they decided, would never catch up. After days of hard riding, it was time to rest.

The party was Stockwell's first real chance to escape.

The Indians danced late into the night around their fire. Maybe it was the flames that gave them the idea.

They decided to burn some of their prisoners. Three of them would die that night. The idea swept through the camp. Some Indians went out for bark to build a new fire. They chose Stockwell and two other prisoners.

Then, just as suddenly as the idea had come, the Indians decided to wait. Maybe they were tired from the dancing. They would let the morning come, they decided, before the executions. The Indians lay down on the ground and quickly went to sleep.

Stockwell was wide-awake. They had forgotten to tie him down.

He had expected to be staked. He lay waiting, but no one came and the camp quieted down. He stood up. No one moved. He could do anything he wanted.

What do you suppose he did? Stockwell waited and thought, standing near the wavering light of the campfire. He was probably picturing the hideous fire planned for the next morning. But what should he do? He had trouble making up his mind.

Finally, he did *something*. He went out in the woods and gathered up wood to feed the dying campfire. Maybe he felt he needed the light to think. Maybe he wanted to see if the Indians were watching him. Whatever his reason, no one stirred.

Then he got a bold idea. He crept around the camp picking up weapons. He hid them together in a pile.

Then he lost his courage.

Carefully he crept back to the hiding place. He picked up all the guns and hatchets he had stolen and took them back to their owners. They never woke up. Then Stockwell lay down, wondering what would happen to him next.

At dawn, there was another argument. Stockwell's masters had decided they didn't want him burned. He was their property, after all, like a horse or a house. Finally the other Indians agreed. There would be no burning of Englishmen that day.

Stockwell had a second chance to get away a few days

later. His three masters had gone hunting. Stockwell had
been left with another brave who suddenly got so sick he
was unable to carry his gun and hatchet. Stockwell helped
out by carrying them for the Indian. Again, the old dream
sprang to mind. He could take the weapons and run.

And then again it didn't seem like such a good idea. Maybe
the Indians would punish the remaining prisoners for Stockwell's escape. Maybe . . .

So Stockwell waited some more, and did what he was told.

The march continued to the north. The Indians and their
prisoners had gone about two hundred miles into what is
now Canada when food began to run low. It snowed or
rained every day. The braves had trouble hunting. They
came to Quinton Stockwell and ordered him to pray for
food.

So Stockwell prayed. He doesn't tell us exactly what he
said. But he probably didn't ask for much: a little meat
from a moose, bear, or raccoon.

Next day, the Indians were able to shoot some bears. But
Stockwell got no thanks for his prayers. Indians ate most of
the meat. Stockwell was forced to eat decayed wood fried
in bear grease.

One night they gave him raccoon grease for supper. He
was starving. His clothes were hardly enough to keep him
warm. His feet were numb. "So I suffered much," he wrote.
"And being frozen was full of pain and could sleep but a
little. Yet must I do my work."

He was hundreds of miles from home. It was a strange
country of frozen lakes and gray, hostile mountains. There
was no hope now that English soldiers would rescue him.

The Indians and their prisoners were now in land controlled by the French, and the French got along with the Indians. Stockwell's feet had been cold so long he could hardly walk. He was sure death was near.

One day, Stockwell was pulling a sled for the Indians when he knew he could go no farther. He stopped. One of his three masters turned on him.

His master shouted at him to move. Stockwell stood still and silent.

The Indian shouted again. He pushed Stockwell backwards onto the ground.

Stockwell said he could do no more.

The Indian threatened to kill him. He pulled out a knife and whipped its point, shining, at Stockwell. He hesitated, then dove at the man on the ground. Stockwell expected to feel the knife plunge into him. He waited for the pain.

It never came. The Indian tore into his clothing. He cut off Stockwell's pockets and ripped away the large pieces of cloth. But he didn't stab his prisoner.

Maybe it was the fact that Stockwell had kept peace between his three masters. Maybe it was the prayers he had said for food. Or the care he had given the sick Indian.

The Indian with the knife didn't explain why, but suddenly he stopped attacking. He put the knife away and carefully wrapped the cloth from Stockwell's pockets around Stockwell's face. It felt warm. Then he gave Stockwell a piece of biscuit as big as a walnut. He told his prisoner to follow him, and began pulling the sled.

Stockwell stood up and tried to follow. But it was hard to walk and the Indian had soon hurried ahead out of sight.

Stockwell kept slipping. Why had he been allowed to live? Where was he going? He staggered on alone, trying to follow his master. It began to get dark.

Suddenly his feet flew out from under him. He landed hard, down again on the ice. He had no strength now to get up. He crawled to a tree.

"And there I lay," Stockwell wrote. "It was now night and very sharp weather. I counted no other but that I must die here."

A voice seemed to come from far away. "Hellooo," it said. Stockwell tried to yell back. It was another Indian, and he was angry. He came closer. He yelled at Stockwell to get up. The nightmare seemed to be starting again.

But Stockwell was ready to die. He couldn't move. Even the threat of death couldn't lift him to his feet.

The second Indian yelled some more. But then, like Stockwell's first master, he suddenly changed. He took off his coat and wrapped Stockwell in it. He left quietly.

In a few minutes, two other Indians returned with a sled. They hauled Stockwell onto it and carried him to a camp. They gave him dry clothes and otter broth.

So that night, the Indians began to care for their captive. For almost three months he had been their slave. Now they served him. They carried him everywhere. They tried to nurse him back to health with Indian remedies. His strange story spread through the French settlement, and at Christmas they brought cake for him to eat.

But Stockwell still wasn't free. Hundreds of miles from home, he couldn't even walk. The Indian medicine didn't work. He was in constant pain. He knew he had only one chance to live: he had to see a French doctor.

It must have taken a lot of courage to ask. Stockwell waited until some Frenchmen were visiting him one day. Then he told one of his masters he wanted to go to the French for help. It was as modest a plea as his prayer for food had been.

But his master was enraged. While Stockwell spoke, the Indian tightened his fingers into a fist. Suddenly he lashed out at Stockwell and hit him on the face. The Frenchmen left abruptly. Stockwell's prayers and pleading seemed useless. After his prayer, there had been a few drops of bear grease. Now there was nothing but pain.

Stockwell was as surprised as the Indians when French soldiers marched into the camp a short time later. They demanded to know who had struck Stockwell. In an instant, they had found his master and arrested him. They told him he would hang.

Why did the French come back? Stockwell's writing doesn't say, and it remains one of the biggest puzzles in his story. Can you think of a good reason? Stockwell couldn't. If one of his masters were hung, he was sure his other two masters would kill him, probably by burning him somewhere faraway in the cold hills.

Stockwell tried to go with the soldiers. They wouldn't let him come, and told him only that the Indians wouldn't dare hurt him now. He was left behind.

Stockwell watched the soldiers go. What could he do to save himself now? The Indians looked coldly at him, crippled, timid, weak, hungry.

He made another decision. It was bolder, in a way, than any he had made since his capture. He told his two remaining masters to pick him up and carry him to the French captain. Stockwell said he would "speak for" his master; he would try to free the man who had held him a slave.

Maybe Stockwell thought hanging was too harsh. Or maybe he figured, desperately, that if he tried again to help, the Indians would let him go without a fight. Whatever the reason, the Indians thought he was crazy. "You are a fool," they told him. The French would hang their prisoner. There was no changing that.

Stockwell pleaded. Finally, the two Indians helped him to the captain's office. And there, Quinton Stockwell, sick and enslaved, begged for the life of his master. It wasn't easy to convince the captain. But finally Stockwell said if the Indian died, other English prisoners might also be killed. The captain wanted no white men killed, even Indian slaves. Finally he agreed to let the Indian go.

Soldiers took the chains off the Indian. And when he heard what Stockwell had done, he ran to him and hugged him. He said Stockwell was a brother. Back at the camp, the other Indians came up to him one by one and shook hands and said, as Stockwell recalled later, "Friend, it is well."

From then on Quinton Stockwell's masters let him go freely to the captain's house. French doctors treated him. It took months to recover, and while he lived with the captain, the Indians seemed to lose interest in him.

Perhaps his timidity had saved his life. If he had run earlier or tried to kill his masters, he could have died in a

gun duel with the Indians, or gotten lost on the strange
wild trails. If he hadn't argued for his master's life, the
Indians might have shot other prisoners and disappeared
with him back into the wilderness. In any number of ways,
he might have died.

But Quinton Stockwell lived. One spring day, one of his
masters came to the captain's house to sell Quinton Stockwell
The Indian needed the money and the captain was willing
to buy his freedom. It was done peacefully on both sides.
The captain paid twenty-one beaver skins. And Quinton
Stockwell, free and perhaps not quite so timid, began the
long trip home.

Chapter 3

Snow-topped Mt. Ararat looms 17,000 feet above the green fields of eastern Turkey, close to the border of Soviet Russia. The story begins with simple faith: three Americans who climbed the mountain believed that somewhere up in that dead snow and ice, thousands of feet above any living tree, there was an ancient wooden boat that had once saved all the land animals of the world—including mankind.

The Bible describes the boat as a kind of barge, about 450 feet long, 75 feet wide, and 45 feet high. That, according to biblical tradition, was big enough to carry representatives of all land animals when God sent floodwaters over the earth. A man named Noah built the ark, the Bible says. The boat floated, with the animals aboard, for five months. Then it landed on "the mountains of Ararat." Noah and his family and all of the animals descended the mountain, leaving the ark above them.

Is it there today? Roger Losier, John Morris, and John Bultema wanted to find out. The three were members of a team backed by a large church in California. The church members believe that the biblical story is true, that the ark is up there somewhere.

Others disagree. Some say the story is only poetry. Some argue that even if the ark did land there, it would have disintegrated by now.

But over the years, the mountain has yielded enough maddening scraps of evidence to keep faith alive. Pictures have shown rectangular objects nestled among rocks. Some explorers report seeing dark, massive forms locked into the glacial ice. Some have found rust red wood high above the line where trees can grow. Perhaps earlier explorers carried the wood up the mountain. Perhaps the forms are simply more rocks. Perhaps not.

Losier, Morris, and Bultema set out to find some hard answers in August of 1972. It had taken months of preparation. They had bought packaged food made for trips into the wilderness. They had learned to climb mountains by practicing on peaks such as Mt. Hood in Oregon. But no practice could have prepared them for what happened.

On August 2, the three young men rode horses up Mt. Ararat until it got too high for the animals. About two miles up, the three dismounted and sent their animals away, along with a local guide boy. They were on their own. They made camp on a strip of ice jutting down the mountain like a knife, and waited for the morning. Their hopes were high that they would find the remains of Noah's ark at the top of the strip of ice.

Early on August 3, they broke camp and began to climb, challenging old Ararat. The mountain seemed to fight back.

The first hint of trouble was a faint rumble up the mountain. Within a second a rock as big as a human head shot past Morris. It whistled angrily as it passed, and sped away. Then came dozens more from above, like bowling balls flying low down the icy alleyway. All the rocks seemed aimed at Losier, Morris, and Bultema. They dropped their packs, all the expensive gear they had collected for months. They ran to the side of the ice, out of the path of the rushing rocks.

The boulders sped over their packs where they had been standing seconds before. Their lives saved, they waited for their equipment to get crushed by the attacks from above.

The fatal blow never came. Miraculously, the rocks missed. When the rockslide stopped a minute later, the packs were safe.

But the mountain still seemed angry. As the three began the climb on the icy trail again, Ararat hurled more rocks down at them. Again they stepped off the trail and survived, and again began the climb. The attacks continued all morning and the climbers fell into a grim rhythm: climb and duck and watch the deadly rocks whistle by. Climb and duck. The ice got steeper and they found it hard to walk. Climb and duck. Slip and drive. And then in the early afternoon when it began to snow, at 13,000 feet, the climbers heard something astonishing.

Far out of contact with the world below, they heard a store-bought whistle. There was someone else on the mountain.

The whistle sounded again. And there, less than 100 yards away, they saw a man. He was yelling at them in a language they couldn't understand. But one thing about him was easily understood. He had a gun. The gun was pointed right at the three climbers.

It was clear that whoever he was, he wanted the three to get off the mountain. Morris tried to tell the man that the climbers had a right to be up there. But it didn't sound convincing. The stranger raised his gun. He looked as if he were going to shoot.

Morris tried to walk closer. The man waved him away.

It was hard to know what to do. If the climbers went back home now, they would waste months of hard preparation and thousands of dollars. But it seemed impossible to talk with the gunman. Morris made up his mind almost immediately, and the other two agreed. All at the same time, the three turned their backs on the man and began to continue up the slope. They were daring the stranger to shoot them in the back. Slowly, step after step, they increased the distance between them and the nozzle of the gun.

The shots never came. The man disappeared like a ghost somewhere below them. They never saw him again.

It was to be their last warning before the storm hit hard. Snow swirled about their legs, hiding their feet and ankles. It got so heavy no one could see. The climbers decided to tie themselves together with rope so no one would get lost. The temperature dropped. The snow got deeper.

Then the lightning began. "There were flashes all around us," Losier said when I interviewed him. "The electricity made my hair stand on end. I thought, 'Man, I've got an Afro haircut.' Lightning seemed to go through everything. It made my ice ax sing. You could feel the vibrations.

"It was scary, but it was an unusual kind of fear," Losier said. "I kept thinking, 'Maybe I'll be hit,' but there was nothing I could do about it." The air on the mountain buzzed. Thunder roared warning.

Morris thought the only hope of survival was to keep climbing up into the storm, trying to reach a flat section in the ice. But Bultema was tired. He headed for a large rock, sat down, and began to take his pack off. Morris began to warn him to get away from the rock. It was too late.

The lightning hit with full force. As Morris remembers it, the electricity seemed to pin Bultema back against the rock. His arms and legs stuck straight out into the air. The same bolt flipped Morris and Losier off the rock and down the slope. Bultema struggled like a trapped animal to get his feet down on the ground. Finally a foot made contact. Instantly, he too was thrown down somersaulting into the snow.

Losier said he didn't recall being hit. He had been thrown farther down the hill—about fifty feet—than any of the three, and had struck his head on something as he fell. Now he couldn't remember why he was there. He began to climb slowly back toward two white figures he saw in the snow.

"What are we doing here?" he asked them. He was angry they weren't giving sensible answers. Looking for an *ark?* Hit by lightning? Why was everybody lying around? Why didn't everybody go get shelter under that big rock above?

In another place and time it might have been funny. Losier was acting like a clown. But there was blood on his head. Morris was sure Losier was seriously hurt, thousands of feet above help.

Bultema and Morris could think normally, but clear thinking wasn't enough. Bultema thought his leg was broken. Morris found he couldn't move his legs. He knew that unless the three could get out of the storm they would freeze to death within a couple of hours.

At first, he decided he was sure to die. He began to think about what it would be like. Because he was a strongly religious person, he decided it wouldn't be so bad. He hoped death would come quickly to spare him pain.

Then he remembered the job he felt called to do. He thought of the people who had given him support, in California, and of the little miracles that had brought the three climbers far above the clouds, still alive despite all the mountain could throw at them.

He decided he wanted to live. He began rubbing his numb legs. Slowly, a burning sensation grew until it hurt so much he had to try to put it out with snow.

He could *feel* again. A half hour later, his knees could bend. In an hour came another miracle. He could walk.

Morris worked his way slowly over to Bultema and began to rub his legs. The ankle didn't seem broken after all, although Bultema still couldn't move. And Losier still wasn't making any sense.

Losier sat on a rock talking like a baby. He was shaking with cold and didn't know what to do about it.

"I needed warmth and didn't know it," he said. Finally, Morris and Bultema tried the only medicine they had: they got mad.

"After a lot of baby talk, they blew up at me," Losier said.

Morris angrily opened Losier's pack and pulled out warm clothes. Like a scolding parent, he pushed Losier's arms and legs into heavy parkas, nylon pants, and a waterproof poncho. As Morris finished, Losier suddenly seemed to come to.

The climbers were recovering. They were still alive. But they were far from safe. Lightning still buzzed and crackled around them. Winds whipped snow into angry, stinging clouds. None of the three had much strength, and for now the only safe place to go was higher up, to a flat shelf on the ice where the climbers might—if the miracles could hold out—put up a tent.

No one could see more than ten feet in any direction. Morris and Losier struggled upward, leaving Bultema to try to rub his legs back to life. The pair found a path. But it ran almost straight up and footing was terrible.

Finally the slope broke, the ground leveled. There was a place for a tent. The two helped Bultema up the steep path and almost as soon as the three climbers reached the flat spot again, the storm ended. The tent went up easily. They had a hot dinner, sang, and said prayers.

As soon as he could, Morris slipped away under a clear sky and took binoculars to the edge to a place where he could see back down the mountain. Carefully he searched over all the land below. He didn't see the ark or anything like it.

Strength returned to the climbers. They continued to search up on Ararat for two more days before coming down safely. They found no shreds of wood, no clear evidence that Noah had once landed there.

They had to settle for coming down the mountain with their lives.

Chapter 4

Lifeboat in Space

The spaceship carrying three men to the moon shuddered as if it had bumped into something.

The shudder made no sense. There was nothing to bump into, 205,000 miles away from earth in black space. Astronaut Fred W. Haise was floating between two cabins in the ship when he felt the bump. He pulled himself quickly into the main cabin, called the command module. The ship continued to shake up and down. Haise's heart was beating twice as fast as usual.

There was no gravity in space, so Haise appeared to be floating through the air. Quickly he pulled himself to his seat. Another astronaut, John L. Swigert, slammed the door shut, sealing off the cabin.

Now all three were sitting in a small compartment, about as big as a three-man tent. It was a little after 9:00 P.M.

on Monday, April 13, 1970, somewhere between earth and the moon.

Sealed into their cramped quarters, the men tried to figure out what had happened by reading dials in front of them. The whole ship was wobbling now, something like a car with a flat tire. The men's eyes raced over the lighted boards.

A few of the dials were behaving wildly. Some showed the ship was losing electrical power. Capt. James A. Lovell tried to stop the wobbling by firing small rockets outside the ship. It didn't work. Then suddenly he hit on the problem. One of the instruments was like a fuel gauge on a car. It showed how much fuel—called oxygen—was left in one of the large tanks. The fuel was used to make electrical power to run the ship. Just as important, it helped fuel the men: oxygen was a vital part of the air they breathed. Without fuel, the ship—and the men running it—would die.

Lovell radioed the earth about what he had found. "Our oxygen number two tank is reading zero," he said.

Then Lovell got out of his seat and glided to a window so he could see the outside of Apollo 13. He turned to the section of the ship called the service module. That was a large cylinder containing the fuel tanks and the main rocket engine. The service module was connected to one end of the command module where the men lived. In the black night of space, Lovell saw a ghostly cloud coming out of the side of the service module.

Lovell got back on the radio, flashing the news to the gray-walled mission control room in Texas. "It looks to me that we are venting something," he said.

The ship, Apollo 13, pride of America, had soared into the sky two days before. Now like an old boat it was leaking, or "venting." One of its round, silvery fuel tanks had exploded, blasting a hole right through the side of the service module. Fuel was disappearing into space. Every two sec-✈ onds the ship moved a mile closer to the moon, farther from earth.

Dozens of people on the ground tried to figure out what to do. What they needed was a lifeboat, another rocket ship with its own supply of oxygen, its own rocket engine, to bring the men home.

Well, in a way, Apollo 13 had a lifeboat. Its name was Aquarius. Aquarius was a small but complete rocket ship attached to the command module where the men lived. It had been designed to break away from the command module and carry two men to the surface of the moon, and then back up to the command module. It had its own air supply. It had its own rocket engine.

What it didn't have was space. There was no room to sit down in Aquarius. It had about as much space as a small closet. Aquarius also lacked strength. It was built to land on the moon—not on the earth. If the astronauts tried to ride it all the way home into the earth's air, it would burn to cinders. The command module was the only part of Apollo 13 designed to survive the fiery plunge back to earth.

The people on the ground argued and sweated over what to do. Finally, they agreed on a plan. They radioed the idea into space: Turn off everything in the command module to save what fuel is left. Climb into Aquarius. Use the Aquarius air supply and the Aquarius rocket to get home.

Then when you get close to earth, climb back into the command module to protect yourselves when things get hot during landing.

Haise was the first to enter Aquarius. There were no lights except his flashlight. He floated into the dark little cabin. Closer and closer he moved to instruments covering the walls, closer to two triangular windows that had been designed for a view of the moon's surface. There were no seats. Haise turned on some of the switches. Soon the cramped lifeboat was filling with its own supply of oxygen.

Lovell joined Haise. Swigert stayed behind in the command module for a few minutes. He turned everything off, saving the little fuel left for the earth landing. Then he followed the other two into Aquarius. There was no chance now that Aquarius would land on the moon. It now had a new mission, a more important one: to keep three men alive.

Apollo 13, its crew huddled in one end, hurtled on toward the moon. The ship curved around the back side of the moon, out of sight of the earth. The gray lunar surface, pocked with craters, unrolled beneath the ship at about ten times the speed of a fast jet plane on earth. Then the earth, a blue green ball, appeared again. It was time to see whether the small rocket on Aquarius could blast the whole ship into a good course back home to Earth. If the course adjustment failed, Apollo could miss the earth completely. The crew wouldn't survive long, and the ship would carry their bodies on an endless trip through space.

"Mark!" said a man in Texas, telling Lovell he had forty seconds to go before firing. Lovell put his hand on the firing button. "Five . . . four . . . three . . . two . . . one."

At exactly the right time, the rocket began to fire. No one could hear the explosion. Sound couldn't pass through empty space. But the astronauts could feel the movement. The little rocket on Aquarius kept pushing the whole ship into line. It fired on, a four-minute explosion. Then a computer took over. It turned the rocket off at precisely the right instant.

Men in space and on the ground anxiously checked the course. The rocket had done its job. The ship was aimed for a landing in the Pacific Ocean, a quarter of a million miles away. At least the ship was headed in the right direction. Whether it would splash down safely, no one knew.

Other problems crowded in on the men in the crippled ship.

Since fuel was low, there was not enough energy to keep Aquarius warm. The temperature was dropping. And there were no winter clothes on Apollo 13.

Fuel had been used to make water, so now water supplies were low, too. Like desert explorers, the men had carried some of the water from the main supply in the command module to Aquarius in plastic juice bags. But the supply was still low. Their constant thirst was making it hard for the men to concentrate.

The air was bad. Back in the command module, a machine cleaned the air of dangerous gases. Aquarius had no such machine. Scientists on the ground suggested that the men try to build an air cleaner out of scraps aboard the ship—plastic bags, a hose, some cards, and tape. No one knew whether the contraption would work.

By now, millions of people on earth were worried

about the voyagers from the moon. Concern had spread around the world. Thirteen countries offered to help in recovering the ship if it made it back to earth. People gathered on streets to watch TV reports, and in churches and synagogues to pray.

In space, it was cold and quiet. By early Wednesday morning, the temperature in Aquarius had dropped to fifty-five degrees. No one aboard could sleep. The men stayed awake, thirsty, tired, cold, moving around restlessly like animals in a small cage.

"You got up kind of early, didn't you?" the ground radioed. The men said it was impossible to sleep. Temperatures were headed for the forties.

The air got worse. Before noon on Wednesday, a yellow light in Aquarius warned suddenly that it wasn't safe to breathe. Lovell turned on the taped-up contraption. It began to suck air through the filter.

Clean air flooded the cabin. The light went off. They would be okay as long as the makeshift air cleaner worked.

The double impact of thirst and cold was making it ever more difficult to think. At one point, Lovell was looking out the window. "The moon passed by," he said, watching a ball move slowly in front of the window. Then he corrected himself. "No, that's the earth." For an instant, the astronaut hadn't been able to tell them apart.

A sharp mind was now critical. The ship bore in on the earth like a bullet. The men had to begin moving back into the command module to prepare to land. Landing was complicated because most of Apollo 13 had to be thrown away in space before it was safe to come down. The command module had a solid round shield on its bottom to help it survive the heat when it plunged into the earth's air. The service module and Aquarius had no such protection. One of the astronauts' first jobs was to separate the command module from Aquarius and the service module.

The service module was the first to go. Explosive charges pushed it away from the command module. The module was spinning away into space when Lovell spotted the damage caused by the fuel tank explosion. "There's one whole side of that spacecraft missing," he said. Haise saw it too. "It's really a mess," he reported. The service module shrank to a dot in the blackness.

As it disappeared in the distance, the crew aboard Apollo began to worry about something else, more dangerous than anything that had happened. The fuel tank explosion had damaged the service module just a few feet from the heat shield that would protect the men during the last few minutes of the flight. Suppose the explosion had also damaged the heat shield. Would the command module stand the shock of re-entering Earth's atmosphere? No one talked about the possibility. The earth seemed to grow steadily, a big, blue ball out the spaceship's window.

Lovell was the last to leave Aquarius. By the time he had eased his way back through a tunnel into the command module, Aquarius was filled with debris from the flight. The men switched over to the remaining oxygen in the command module. They sealed off the compartment in Aquarius. Then they blasted away from their lifeboat.

They were falling now, in the command module cone, at about 15,000 miles an hour. In less than an hour, they would either land, or burn up.

No one was talking much. Men on the ground were plot-

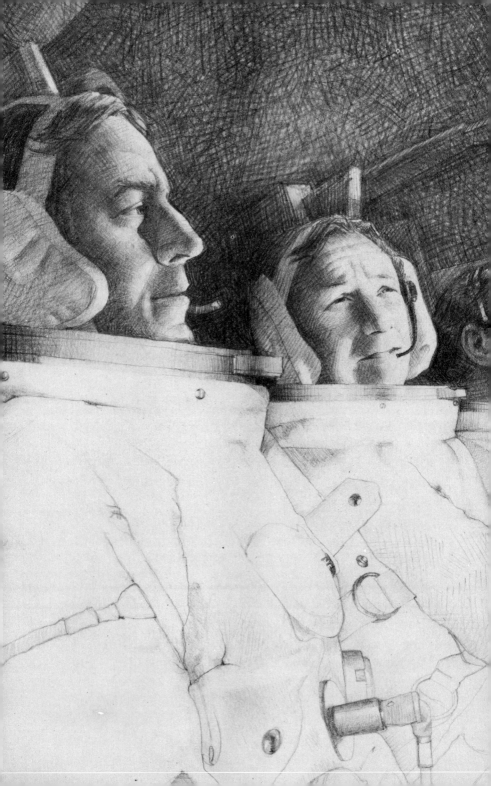

ting the cone's course. There was little that could be done now. The command module was picking up speed. 17,000 miles an hour. 18,000. In a few minutes it reached 20,000 miles an hour. That meant the end of radio contact was near. The ship-to-ground radios couldn't work through the fire that would soon surround the command module. People on the ground talked nervously with the astronauts about a party they would have after the mission was ended. Swigert said he wished he could be there for it.

About 400,000 feet above the earth, the capsule began heating up. Soon flames whipped around it and the radio went dead. Ground scientists expected radio contact to be broken for about three and a half minutes.

But at the end of three and a half minutes, there was still no word. Another half-minute ticked by. Apollo 13 remained silent. And then another half-minute. Some people began to lose hope.

"Okay, Joe." The voice was Swigert's. He was on the air again. Within minutes, white-and-orange parachutes rose like giant party balloons over the little command module. It splashed into the sea and the men were picked up from their bobbing ship, still so cold inside you could see your breath. They had survived.

And what of Aquarius? The lifeboat had continued to send radio signals long after it had been separated from the men it had saved. "Where did she go?" one of the astronauts had asked just before radio contact was broken.

"Oh I don't know," replied one of the ground crew. "She's up there somewhere." A radio aboard the deserted lifeboat sputtered out one dying signal. Then lifeboat Aquarius plunged into the earth's atmosphere and burned to ashes.

Chapter 5

The Island Ghost of World War II

The day Hiroo Onoda went to war against the Americans, his  mother gave him a sword. "Die well," she told her son.

Onoda, a Japanese soldier, carried the sword to a small island named Lubang in the Pacific Ocean. His orders were simple. It was 1944 and the Japanese were losing the war. Americans were expected to land on Lubang any time. Onoda's orders were to fight the Americans.

He set up camp in the jungle on the island a few days after Christmas, 1944. Then he and other soldiers waited. They had a good supply of bullets. And Onoda had his sword and faith in his mission. Months passed. The Americans dropped the first atomic bombs on two Japanese cities in 1945, and the Imperial Japanese Army ordered its soldiers to give up. The war ended.

The world began to recover. Japan began to rebuild. Most Americans came home. Men who had hit the beaches of

Pacific islands in war now had time to rest in the sun of American beaches. Former soldiers built houses, went back to school, learned to enjoy newfangled inventions like television.

The people who lived on Lubang, meanwhile, tried to get back to farming. The problem was that Hiroo Onoda had never gotten orders to stop fighting. Hiroo Onoda and his comrades were still at war. Like a sudden storm, they would swoop out of the jungle. They would burn crops and houses, shoot farmers, then disappear into the jungle for safety.

The soldiers could survive in the jungle. There were plenty of bananas and coconuts, and they could steal rice, salt, and other food from villages.

Years went by. Farmers lived in terror. Many refused to work the land near the mountains because they were sure they would be shot by the hidden Japanese gunmen in the jungle. The farmers were right to be frightened: almost every harvest season, someone would be hit. Scores of people were wounded. Many died.

Ten years passed after Onoda made his landing. Japanese officials had identified the soldiers on Lubang. Everyone knew Onoda and his comrades were fighting their own war. No one knew how to get word to them to stop.

The Japanese dropped leaflets and pictures on the island. The leaflets announced the end of the war, and the pictures showed Onoda's family. Onoda thought it was all a trick by the Americans. In 1959, the Japanese even sent Onoda's brother Toshio to the island to try to call the soldier home.

Toshio used a loudspeaker to broadcast his voice over the

jungle territory. "Please come out where we can see you," he said. Onoda heard the voice. But he didn't believe it was Toshio. He was sure it was just an actor pretending to be his brother.

On his last day on the island, Toshio tried desperately to get through to Onoda. Through the loudspeaker, he began singing a song he knew Onoda liked. Onoda listened, hidden about 150 yards away. He was beginning to believe it was his brother. Then Toshio's voice tightened and grew higher. The tune went sour. Onoda laughed. Now he was certain it had been an act.

But it had not been an act. While he was singing, Toshio had realized it was his last chance to get through to his brother. He had choked up and lost his voice. A short time later, he left Lubang.

After the search in 1959, Japanese officials decided the soldiers must be dead. So Onoda was declared officially dead. But then he swept out of the jungle again. More searchers looked for him and couldn't find him. Once again officials decided he was dead. Once again the "dead" Onoda came out of the jungle to fight the farmers.

In 1972, 13,000 men blanketed Onoda's jungle home. They were convinced they had looked everywhere. The search cost $375,000. The result: nothing. But Onoda fought on.

Over the years, Onoda's comrades did turn up. Two were killed by Filipino patrols, and one gave himself up. But the island ghost of World War II laid low. He might have spent the rest of his life at war. It seemed impossible to get word to

him. He did steal a transistor radio in 1965, but heard nothing on it to make him think he should quit. Thousands of searchers hadn't been able to find him.

Finally, one man did. The man who ended Onoda's war was a twenty-four-year-old former student named Norio Suzuki. Suzuki pitched a little tent on Lubang in February 1974, and waited for Onoda to appear. One evening, while Suzuki was building a fire, Onoda crept into his camp, ready to kill him.

Suzuki raised his hands. Onoda saw his knees were shaking. "I'm Japanese," Suzuki said. "I'm Japanese. I'm Japanese." Onoda questioned him, suspicious. After a long talk, he began to believe Suzuki, to believe there was a slight chance the war was really over.

Why? It's not clear in any news reports, or even in Onoda's own account. There were probably a few reasons why he believed Suzuki. Onoda's last comrade had been shot dead two years before. He was lonely, and it was good to talk to anyone from his country. Suzuki told Onoda about how he had wandered all over the world, working his way through fifty countries in four years. He reminded Onoda of the way he had been thirty years before. Onoda liked him. And he liked the sweetened beans Suzuki offered him. For the first time in three decades, Onoda felt he was eating decent food. He told Suzuki he might be ready to stop fighting.

But there was one problem. Suzuki wasn't a soldier. He had no power to order Onoda to lay down his sword. Onoda had remained a good soldier and he wanted orders.

So Suzuki went back to Japan. He found Onoda's commander, Yoshimi Taniguchi, a former major who had become a book dealer. Taniguchi agreed to help. He and Suzuki went back to Lubang and talked Onoda out of the jungle. They discussed the surrender for a while. Then Onoda returned to one of his hideouts. He had to get his sword.

The formal surrender was arranged for March 10, 1974. He came out of the jungle wearing his patched Japanese army uniform. He was freshly shaved except for a small mustache and beard. His hair was clipped short. He stood straight and proud. He offered his old sword to a Filipino soldier who returned it to him. And he met his brother, Toshio.

"I am sorry I have disturbed you for so long a time," reporters heard him tell Toshio. His brother put both hands on Onoda's shoulders.

"You did well," he said.

Onoda came home a free man a few days later. The president of the Philippines had given him a full pardon. The president had hugged him and said he admired his courage, and returned the sword to him again. Now Onoda stepped off the plane and picked up his baggage, including his rifle, ammunition, and the sword. His mother, eighty-eight years old, was waiting for him in a wheelchair.

"I'm so happy to see you come home alive," she said. "You did a fine job."

Not everyone agreed. Back in Lubang, he had left thirty dead. Even some Japanese said Onoda was like a lot of Japanese soldiers in World War II. They would follow any order, to the death, even if the orders were wrong. After he'd gotten home, Onoda was a hero to some of his countrymen. He embarrassed others.

But no matter how his countrymen felt about him, he raised a question: How many ghosts on other islands were still holding out? How many Japanese were waiting, cleaning their guns, waving rusty swords, for the Americans to attack?

Chapter 6

Graves for the Living

Levi Milley thought it was too nice a day to go to work. It was sunny the afternoon of Thursday, October 23, 1958. So Milley didn't look forward to starting his afternoon shift thousands of feet beneath the earth in the coal mines.

Springhill, Nova Scotia, in the southeastern corner of Canada, depended on the mine for money. It had for ninety years. But the price for chipping at the rich veins of black coal had been high. At least two men a year died from accidents in the tunnels burrowed below the ground. Major disasters—fires, massive collapse of tunnels—had taken 164 lives.

The work was dangerous, and hard. At the entrance to the mine, men like Milley traded street clothes for work uniforms that could never be completely scrubbed clean of coal dust. They slid battery-powered lamps into helmets and rode small railroad cars down a steep incline into the earth.

The temperature rose as they traveled to work. It was never cooler than eighty degrees in the mine, even in winter. Once at work, the men chopped away the walls of coal. The warm air filled with black dust. The men took off their shirts. Dust worked its way into the pores of their skin. Dust filled their lungs and turned them black. Most miners had red welts on their bodies caused by the irritating dust. In exchange for their labor, the miners earned about eleven dollars a day.

Around six in the evening of October 23, Milley and the others stopped for dinner. Levi had brought a couple of hard-boiled eggs and bran muffins in his food pail.

At seven, the ground under their feet shook a little. Miners called that a bump. It was caused by the sudden shifting of coal under pressure. Bumps could be dangerous. Ceilings could collapse. But the bump at seven was gentle. The miners kept working.

It was 8:06 P.M. An unidentified miner later told a government investigator what had happened.

He was talking with another miner about the tremor an hour before. He asked if the other man had felt the bump.

"And just as I said 'bump,' that is when the big one came," the miner recalled. "It seemed like the word 'bump' was the trigger.

"Immediately I said that, why, he flew. I seen him going. I seen his feet. That was all. I thought that the roof had come in on us."

It had. Major parts of the mine were collapsing in a fraction of a second. The explosive movement of the earth tossed men around like rag dolls. Dozens were buried and crushed instantly. The upheaval in the tunnels was so violent, ground shook eight hundred miles away. People on the surface in Springhill were knocked to the floor of their homes.

"It just felt like the whole world hit the house," one woman told investigators. "It was terrific. I knew it was a bump, and I thought of my husband in the mine, and I said right out loud, 'My God, it happened.'"

Within minutes, miners on the surface—resting in Springhill after their shifts—came running to the mine entrance. Everyone was confused. A nurse in her home felt the ground shake. She knew instantly what had happened below, and she broke out crying. She hurried to the mine where someone, probably in a daze, told her everything was going to be all right. The nurse went home to bed, then got up again, got dressed, and went to the hospital. She knew everything was not going to be all right.

When the mine began churning, Milley flew into the air. Flipping head over feet, he hit the roof of the tunnel, then dropped back to the floor. He was still conscious. Pressure beneath the floor had pushed it up to the ceiling. The chamber wherc Levi lay was now only three feet high.

Other miners cried around him in the darkness. Coal and rock continued to shift around in the tunnels. Someone nearby called for help. Milley turned his head light on and dragged himself toward the call. He found a miner whose leg was trapped under rock. Milley helped him free the leg. Then the two men continued to move around, looking for others, tracking the sounds of crying and praying. They found some miners with broken bones, others too shocked to talk; some—miraculously—seemed unhurt. Milley called on everyone

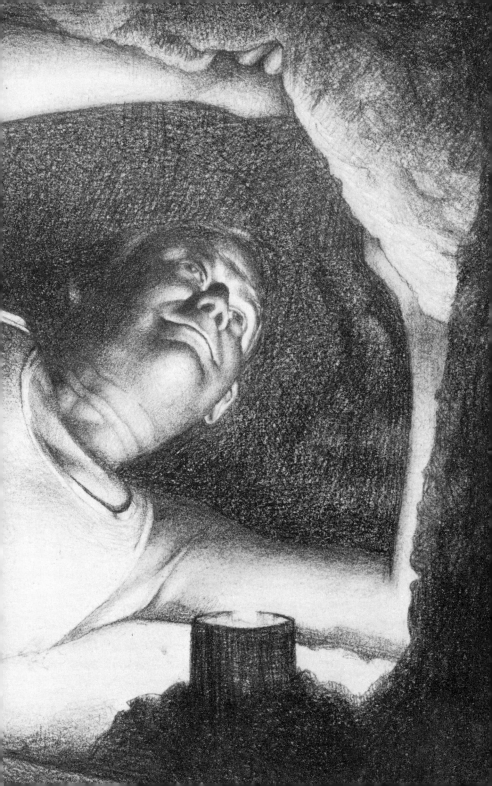

who could hear him to speak their names. Eleven men answered.

Miners who could move around looked for a way out. The ceiling was just high enough for them to walk, bent over. They found bodies scattered on the floor, a few sandwiches, some water and aspirin, but they found no openings in the solid, rocky wall.

One of the twelve survivors, Wilfred Hunter, discovered a body hanging down from the ceiling. The body looked familiar. Hunter was certain it was his younger brother, Frank, another miner. Hunter spoke to the lifeless form. "I'm sorry," he said.

But Wilfred Hunter was wrong. The body was not his brother's. Frank Hunter was alive, too. He and seven other men were trapped in another chamber. The two brothers were only a few hundred feet apart. The distance might as well have been miles: a solid wall of rock and coal separated them.

The two small chambers had enough dank air and food scraps to support the twenty survivors for a short time. But in other ways, the men were already living in graves, buried thousands of feet below Springhill, separated from the open tunnels to the surface by hundreds of feet of fallen earth. No one above knew where they were.

Within the first day after the upheaval in the mine, 81 of the 174 men on the afternoon shift had been rescued alive. But teams of diggers carrying tanks of oxygen to breathe had found many bodies as well. One of the rescuers later described what it was like to make narrow tunnels into the debris, looking for other miners.

"Four of us spelled one another off," he said. "I'd go in there first on my stomach and dig . . . maybe for two minutes, maybe for five, maybe ten—no longer than ten. There wasn't the right air for you . . . And then, it was so dusty. The minute you stuck a pick in it, you got that dust and sometimes you could hardly see. I'd come out and the other fellow would crawl in over my back and go in and dig.

"You had to dig each body out. Maybe strike a boot toe first, maybe strike a cap first . . . My buddy took so sick he had to go home."

By Monday morning in Springhill, more than three days after the disaster, the manager of the mine company prepared for a press conference. His message was stark. There was little hope that anyone else could be alive in the mine.

A reporter who had gone to Springhill to cover the conference met a small unidentified boy walking aimlessly around the mine grounds. The reporter asked what the trouble was. "I'm looking for my daddy," the boy said. The reporter asked where the boy's father was. "He's in the mine," the boy said. "He hasn't come up yet." The reporter told the boy it would be better if he went home.

"No, no," the boy said. "I don't want to go home. Everybody's crying there."

At about the time that conversation took place, the group of eight men trapped thousands of feet below was celebrating a birthday. It was a grim celebration. Garnet Clarke was twenty-nine years old, and he told another miner, Maurice Ruddick, that he thought it was going to be his last birthday.

But Ruddick hadn't lost his spirit. He woke up the others, including Frank Hunter, and told them they were going to celebrate. He found the last sandwich and broke it into grimy pieces and told the others to pretend it was cake. Then he passed around the water can. Each man wet his lips. By the time Ruddick got the can back, there were only a few drops left. He finished the drops. For a few seconds, it seemed to be the end of the party. Then Ruddick began singing.

"Happy birthday to you, Happy birthday . . ." No one else sang. Ruddick stopped and told everyone to join him. Then he began singing again, and the others added ragged voices. In the darkness blanketing his birthday party, Garnet Clarke was crying.

The following day, five days after the disaster, Clarke broke off a small piece of wood from one of the timbers used to hold up the roof. He put the piece in his mouth and chewed it over and over until it was soft enough to swallow. The others did the same thing. There was nothing else to eat. Late that day, one of the men died. And then there were seven.

A few hundred feet away, the group of twelve was giving up hope. They had run out of water a couple of days before. One of them had suggested drinking their own urine. "That is what we have to do," the miner had said. "Drink it, if it makes us sick or not." Using cups, several of the miners first wet their lips. Then they rinsed their mouths, and then drank. Others could never do it.

"I wasn't thirsty," one said later.

Time passed slowly. Hope withered. Then, in the hot darkness, they thought they heard rats, scratching at the walls, getting closer, in rat-sized tunnels, waiting for the miners to die. The noises seemed to be coming from a narrow pipe jutting into the chamber. It had been used to carry fresh air to the miners; now it just looked like a piece of junk sticking out near the floor.

But those noises—what made them? On Wednesday morning, two of the men crawled to the opening of the pipe. They lay side by side, listening to the scratching. The two lay there for hours, their faces a few inches from the opening.

Early in the afternoon, one of the men heard a voice in the pipe.

Barely able to believe his ears, he put his mouth to the opening. He yelled with all his strength. A voice, clear and distant, hollered back. The rescuers had never stopped digging. Now, six days after the mine had caved in, the diggers were less than seventy-five feet away.

It took another twelve hours to burrow to Levi Milley and the eleven others, but in the meantime word had been flashed up through the main tunnel to the families above. It was a miracle: twelve men were alive.

The phone rang at the Milley home around lunchtime, six days after Levi had last gone to work. Milley's sixteen-year-old daughter, Judy, answered it. She and her mother had tried to prepare for the bad news for days. The call was from the minister of their church. He said rescuers had just located twelve survivors. Judy's father was one of them.

Judy Milley was so stunned she didn't know what to say. Her mother had heard her quiet responses to the caller. Mrs. Milley was certain of the worst.

Her daughter ran to the kitchen. "Daddy's alive!" she said. Mrs. Milley opened her arms wide.

Rescuers carried the twelve men to the surface and kept on digging. Two days later came another miracle. At 4:42 A.M. on Saturday, November 1, they found a lone man still alive. "He was in a little wee cubbyhole not higher than the arm of a chair," one of the rescuers said later.

The diggers moved on through a small tunnel until they came to Frank Hunter and the rest of the group of seven. None of the men could stand up, but they cried with joy to see men from the surface. In a few hours they were in hospital beds, safe in Springhill. One of Maurice Ruddick's twelve children crawled into bed next to him. Maurice kissed him.

Five days later, the last of the seventy-four bodies was found; there were no other survivors. And then the mine was sealed off forever.

Chapter 7

The plane plunged into clouds over the Andes mountains. It was hard to see anything through the small windows. But no one thought there was much to worry about. The forty-five people aboard the plane, from the South American country of Uruguay, were having a good time.

Many of them were athletes. They played rugby, a game something like football. Now they were throwing the rugby ball up and down the aisle of the plane. Others played cards. They expected to be on the other side of the mountains and over the green fields of Chile in a few minutes.

Then, in the gloom of the clouds, the plane began to shake. Winds over the mountains were bouncing it around. Some of the passengers laughed nervously. Others continued chatting or tried to read books. Suddenly, the plane dropped several hundred feet. Some of the passengers reached out to hold hands. There was growing fear. Others tried to fight the fear by throwing the ball between the seats as if everything were fine.

The plane dropped again. Now it was below the clouds. And those who looked out the window could see exactly where they were. They were racing by the rocky side of a mountain. The plane soared more than the length of a football field every second. The dark rocks were no more than ten feet from the tip of the wing. Some of the passengers began to pray.

It was too late to do anything. In an instant, the right wing hit the side of the mountain. It flipped back. It smashed through the tail. Then the left wing broke off. Some passengers died right away.

"People who failed to get their seat belts fastened were simply swept out of the hole left when the tail broke off," one passenger said later. "People were screaming. And I could smell fuel and the cold air gushing in from outside."

The plane was coming in like a rocket. Miraculously, the cabin missed the rocks and began skidding into a snowy hill like a ski jumper making a landing. It dug a deep trail down the hill. Snow rushing under the body of the plane slowed it like a brake. Inside, seats were crushed together. The pilot died immediately in the crash. So did thirteen others. The plane bumped hard to a stop.

Those who survived that mountain crash in October 1972, began a fight to live. Their story is one of the most famous of all survival stories.

There are fantastic rumors about what happened on the mountain after the crash. But the true story is fantastic enough. It was told by a British writer, Piers Paul Read, in a book called *Alive*. Survivors approved Read's writing. So with that book, and reliable news reports from the time, we can be almost certain that this is what happened, even though it seems unbelievable.

One of the first to move inside the wrecked plane was Roberto Canessa, a student. Canessa was studying to be a doctor. But he didn't know nearly enough to take care of all the dying people aboard the plane. Canessa moved from person to person. He wiped away blood on a young woman's face. Many others called for help. He moved on. One of his friends, Nando Parrado, was unconscious. Canessa held his wrist. Parrado's heart was beating. But his face was banged up, and covered with blood. Canessa didn't think he would live. He kept moving.

Outside the gray scene of mountains and snow began to darken. Night was coming. Some who had survived were hoping rescue helicopters were already on the way. It got darker. No rescuers came.

Canessa was still working hard. As it got colder, survivors crept closer together to warm each other. They rubbed each others' arms and legs to drive away the cold. There were no blankets in the plane. Some of the people had nothing to wear but summer shirts. Canessa discovered that the coverings on the seats came off. He undid the zippers. He passed around the coverings. The others bundled themselves as best they could. The coverings weren't much. The temperature was below zero.

The screaming and moaning never seemed to stop. Cold winds streamed through the hole in the back of the plane. It was hard to think clearly. Some in the plane had wild wide-awake dreams.

One suddenly thought he was in the middle of a city. He

got up and headed for the opening in the back of the plane.
He said he was going to the store to get something to drink.
Another man yelled that someone was trying to kill him.
Snow blown in by the wind began to build up near the hole.
Parrado was still unconscious.

The plane had landed almost exactly in the middle of the
Andes mountains. The mountains run like a spine from north
to south down South America. The plane had been trying to
hurdle the spine, chasing the sun toward the west. It
seemed like many nights before the sun came around to the
east again. Three more died in the darkness.

When morning finally came, Canessa again made rounds
of those still alive. Some didn't know how badly they were
hurt. One of the husky rugby players, Antonio Vizintin, was
dripping blood from his arm. He said it wasn't painful. But
when Canessa tried to take off his coat the clothing stuck to
the arm. Canessa cut the coat away. Blood came rushing out.
The cut was quickly bandaged. But Canessa didn't think
Vizintin would live long.

While they waited for a rescue party, the passengers looked
for food. There wasn't much: a few bars of chocolate and
other candy, dried fruit, crackers, a couple of cans of shell-
fish, some nuts and jam. It might take a few days for help to
come. So they decided to ration the food. Each person would
get only a small amount for each meal. Lunch was a small
piece of chocolate and a few swallows of wine. After lunch
they heard a plane flying somewhere above. Clouds kept
them from seeing the plane. It seemed only a short time
before night fell again.

It was discouraging that another day had gone by without
rescue. But in small ways, the survivors had begun to think

of ways to soften the waiting. The next day they began melting snow for water. They cleaned up the cabin. There were
few complaints about the rationing. And there was good news
about Nando Parrado. He had been unconscious since the
crash. Now, two days later, he woke up. He was confused and
weak, but he had survived. As it turned out later, it was lucky
for the rest on the plane that Parrado was alive.

The days stretched into a week. Still no one came to save
them. Food was running out. There were jobs to do: cleaning
up, melting snow, caring for the injured. And now survivors
found it harder to work. They felt weak. They knew they
would have to find food if they were going to survive much
longer.

It was somewhere around the tenth day after the crash
when some of the survivors began talking openly about an
idea they had kept to themselves. Unless help came quickly,
there was only one way to stay alive.

It was awful to think about.

They would have to eat parts of the bodies of those killed
in the crash.

On the tenth day, all the survivors talked for hours about
the idea. Some thought using the bodies to stay alive was like
a heart transplant: a weak heart is replaced by a strong heart
taken from someone who has just died. Canessa argued that
the group could not give up living when there was a
chance to save themselves. The rations wouldn't give them
enough energy to leave the plane and go for help. The bodies
of their friends, now lying in the snow, could save them.

Others said that if they died, they would want the survivors to use *their* bodies for food.

Slowly, doubts began to disappear. Some held back on making a decision. A few said they saw nothing wrong with the idea, but added they couldn't do it themselves as long as there was any chance of rescue.

Most decided there was no other way. Canessa and a few others went out in the snow. He found one of the bodies and cut into it with a piece of broken glass. It was sickening work. He made twenty small slices, the size of large splinters. Then he went back in the plane and told the others that there was food drying in the sun.

No one followed him back outside. Canessa took one of the pieces in his hand. He prayed he was doing the right thing. His hand wouldn't move. He fought with himself. Finally, he pushed the piece into his mouth and ate it. Others began to follow him, sometimes washing down the strange food with a scoop of snow.

Although it kept the survivors alive, the human food wasn't nearly enough. Everyone continued to lose weight. They dreamt of puddings and soups, oranges and pancakes and milkshakes. They made lists in a notebook of all the restaurants they could think of. They remembered the names of almost 100.

One night more than two weeks after the crash, the survivors were getting ready for bed. It was late afternoon. But light on the mountain disappeared early. Outside it was dim. Everyone crawled into the plane to sleep. Canessa stayed awake for a while thinking about his mother. He was trying to send word to her in his mind. He wanted her to know he was alive. Parrado was lying in the middle of the plane. There were other sleepers to his left and to his right.

One of the survivors, Roy Harley, felt the ground shake slightly. Then he heard the noise of something hit the ground outside. There was no other warning. Harley jumped up to see what was wrong. Immediately he was buried to his waist in snow. Tons of snow rolling down the mountain had battered into the plane. In seconds the deadly snow had poured into the hole in the back of the plane. It had covered almost all of the survivors. Under the cold blanket, they had no way to breathe. It was impossible for them to dig up through the two or three feet to air; the snow gripped their arms and legs like chains.

Another survivor, Jose Inciarte, later told journalist Carlos Benales what it had been like. "We were buried and giving ourselves up to die," he said. "It got me with my hand in front of my face. So I managed to make a little cavity and breathe a bit. I heard screaming. In the snow in front of my face there was a foot. And I bit it to see if the owner was still alive." The toe moved.

"I moved my hand about a bit but couldn't get out. I think it was the worst moment of all because I really gave myself up for lost."

Harley and one or two others who were above the snow in the plane started to dig. Canessa was one of the first to be freed. He joined the frantic work. Everyone knew that those still buried wouldn't be able to live without air for more than a few minutes.

Below the digging, Parrado was unable to move an inch. Snow was crushing his chest. He tried to take tiny breaths. But he soon realized he was dying. He knew he would pass out in a few seconds.

Then someone scooped the snow from his face. He could feel the cold air. He was going to live. The other sleepers to his left and right weren't as lucky. Both smothered before rescuers could dig them out.

Inciarte, meanwhile, had decided like Parrado that he was going to die. "Then suddenly they removed some of the snow. And I got an arm out. They pulled me, and I got the other out. Then I managed to get out and help."

Digging was a nearly impossible job. By the time all had been uncovered, eight more had died.

More snow rumbled over the plane that night. It was completely buried. The air that was left began to go bad. No one knew how deeply the plane was buried. Harley tried to dig up from the hole in one end of the plane. He got nowhere. The snow was too hard and deep. There was hardly any room left inside; snow took up almost all the space. The cramped survivors were quickly seized by a new fear.

Perhaps they were buried too far under to escape.

Parrado found a long pole. He rammed it through the roof of the plane and began working it up through the snow. The others watched. They provided light by flicking on cigarette lighters. It wasn't long before the pole poked up through the snow layer and into the night air. Through the hole, the survivors could see the moon and stars.

It took more than a week to dig out the plane and remake the shelter. In the days following the avalanche, the talk among the survivors had turned more and more to escape from the mountain. The plan was simple: send a small group west toward Chile to bring help.

Sun again shown on the wreck of the plane. And three of

the rugby players were chosen to try to make it out of the mountains. One was Antonio Vizintin. On the night of the crash he had been bleeding so much Canessa thought he would die. Now he was strong. The second member of the team was Parrado. He had been given up for dead after the crash, and nearly smothered in the avalanche of snow. Now he too was healthy. Canessa, the medical student who had acted as doctor for the other two, was the third.

The hard life on the mountains continued to take lives. Several more died in the days after the avalanche. Now there were sixteen left. Two out of every three of the original passengers were gone.

One morning, the small band of people left at the plane watched the three young men struggle off into the snow. The passengers knew their lives depended now on Canessa, Parrado, and Vizintin.

The three began climbing the mountain, toward the west. Snow dragged at their ankles. They had to rest every few yards. Back at the plane, the others watched them struggle up the steep hill. They could still see the climbers at lunch. By evening, the three climbers could still see the plane, now far below them.

The climbers were thinking about what they would see when they got to the top of the mountain. All were hoping that the green fields of Chile would spread out before them on the other side. They pictured there a farmer's house and food and help for friends that they had left behind. Perhaps the nightmare would end in a few hours. The mountain got steeper. At one point, Parrado began climbing up a rock jutting out from the snow. Suddenly he kicked loose a large

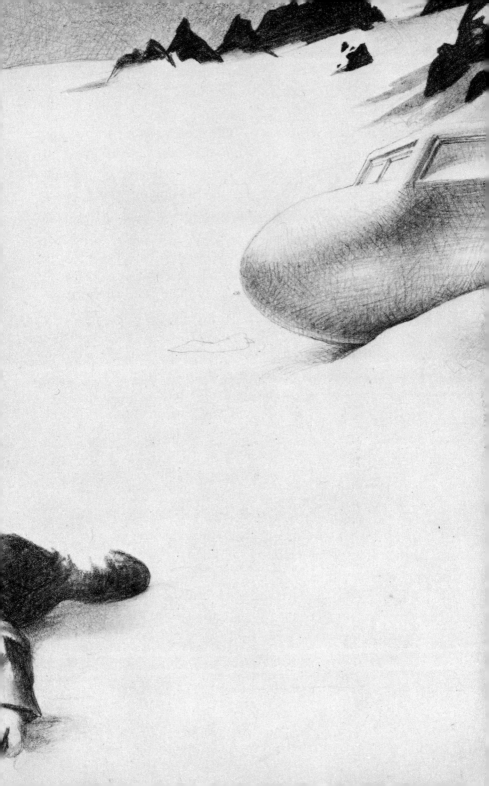

rock. It flew down past Canessa's head. Canessa shouted up at Parrado.

And then he began to cry. The dream seemed impossible.

They spent the first night huddled close together lying on the slanting, ice-cold ground. The climb dragged on through the next morning. The top of the mountain seemed as far away as ever. They still hadn't reached it when night came again.

The next morning, Canessa suggested that Parrado and Vizintin leave their supplies behind and climb ahead to reach the top. The two left immediately. The sky had turned a deep blue. Parrado thought the end of the climb was near. He cut each step into the snow and pulled himself higher. Suddenly the slope leveled off. The climb was over. He was standing on the top, looking over the other side.

What he saw made him sink to his knees.

There were no green fields. No farmhouses. No people to save them. There were just more mountains. Peak after snowy peak, as far as he could see.

Parrado wanted to yell his anger. Nothing came out of his mouth.

For a long time, he looked angrily at the parade of mountains before him. Then he noticed something off to his left that once again raised his hopes. He sent Vizintin back to get Canessa.

Parrado had left clear footholes in the slope and Canessa used them step-by-step to make the climb. He came to the level ground and soon saw the peaks that had driven Parrado to his knees.

"We've had it," Canessa said.

But Parrado pointed off to the left, westward. There, far away, were two unusual mountains. Neither was covered with snow. Perhaps they marked the border of the Andes, Parrado said.

Canessa agreed. But the two peaks looked so far away the three would run out of food long before they got there.

Parrado said they could make the food last much longer if they sent Vizintin back to the plane. Then there would be only two to feed. Canessa agreed again. Within a few hours, Vizintin was on his way back to rejoin the other survivors.

Now it was up to Parrado and Canessa. The two, carrying Vizintin's food as well as their own, struggled off down the other side of the mountain. It took days to get to the bottom. Then came more days of hiking through another snowy valley. Finally, nine days after they had left the plane, they came to a river.

It was about nine in the evening, five days before Christmas, almost seventy days after the plane crash. A Chilean cowboy named Sergio Catalan Martinez was out taking a last look at some of his animals. While he was watching them eat the grass near a rushing river, he thought he heard a faint shouting from the other side. He looked across in the dim light. There were two figures. They were badly dressed. They looked like hoboes. Both of them were shouting and waving. One was kneeling. Whatever it was, Martinez thought, it could wait. He yelled at them that he would be back the next day. He returned to his farm and went to sleep.

The next day, he returned to the river with friends. The two strange figures were still there, still shouting. It was impossible to hear what they were saying. So one of the Chileans threw over a piece of paper wrapped around a rock, and a pen to write with. In a few minutes, a message came flying back over the thirty-five yards of rushing river.

"I come from a plane fallen in the mountains . . ." the message began.

Help came slowly. A few hours later a man on horseback approached Canessa and Parrado and gave them some cheese, then rode off again. After he had left, the two survivors buried the last of the human food they had been carrying. They had no more need for it. That afternoon, the man on horseback took them to a small farmhouse where they ate beans and macaroni and bread and meat scraps until they could hold no more.

It wasn't until the next day that local police arrived. Another day passed before large helicopters arrived and landed. Finally the helicopters, with Parrado riding in one, began the long climb back up into the Andes to the plane. As whirling blades kicked up snow high on the mountains, the fourteen who had been left behind climbed aboard. No one else from the plane would die.

Two years later, some of the survivors made the trip across the mountains to Chile again, to play rugby. But from their point of view there was a big difference this time. They traveled everywhere by bus.

Chapter 8

Do you think you could eat a roasted rattlesnake? How would you feel about a meal of termites and lizards with a side order of frogs? If you were freezing cold in a winter forest, do you think you could force yourself to dig out a hole in the snow and crawl in? Could you drink smelly, muddy swamp water?

What if your life depended on it?

All the survivors in this book did things they never thought they could do. Chances are you could, too. You might even be better at survival than adults.

Let's say a car breaks down in a wilderness, far from any town. What would you do? A lot of adults would leave the car and go for help.

David Eckelberg, a man who teaches air force pilots how to survive if their planes crash, said that youngsters usually know the right thing to do—stay with the car. "Most kids just know they should remain there and wait for help. I've had to search for kids, and usually they'll stay pretty close to the place where they were lost."

Survivors are not supermen or bionic women. People of all ages can muster enough common sense, will, and courage to survive. But there are techniques of survival that can help keep you alive no matter who you are or where you are. Wind-whipped desert sand may sting your face; snowdrifts may drag at your legs, but no matter where you are your physical needs remain the same—you need *shelter, water,* and *food.* Let's look at a few different settings, and see how you can fill those basic needs.

Desert Conditions

Sun rages by day and temperatures over a hundred degrees Fahrenheit wring water from your body. At night it's so cold you shiver. The only sign of life is an occasional lizard or snake; despite shimmering mirages on the sand, no real water is visible. What do you do?

The first thing you **don't** do is move around a lot. If your car has broken down, stay with it. If your plane has crashed, don't leave it now. It's easier for rescuers to spot a car or plane than a person. Besides, your vehicle is your shelter. Hide from the sun under your car, or under a wing of your airplane. If it's daytime and you have no other shelter, dig a ditch—exerting yourself as little as possible—a foot or two deep, preferably in the shade of a shrub. It'll be a lot cooler in the ditch. If you sit on the ground, sit on a couple of shrub branches. If possible, sleep a little off the ground. Remember that snakes, gila monsters and some dangerous lizards feed at night, so if you can, keep a lookout posted. Sleep in shifts if you're with a group. If you take your shoes off at night, shake them out in the morning to remove unfriendly bugs.

Whatever you do, do it slowly and easily. Under normal conditions, your body loses about a quart of water a day through sweating and urinating. But you can easily double that water loss by digging frantically to make shelter, walking, jumping, running, or stripping your clothes off in desert heat. Two or three days of water loss can be enough to kill you.

Water is a critical need. How do you find it in the middle of a desert? Start with your car if you have one. Your car's cooling system is filled with water. It's drinkable as long as it has no antifreeze in it. You can get at it by unscrewing the cap to your radiator near the front of your car just under the hood.

Remember, too, that there is water in the desert if you know how to look. One source is the cactus plant. The cactus spreads its roots out near the surface. When it rains, these roots soak up the water. A cactus can absorb enough water from just one rainstorm to last a whole year.

The squat, rounded barrel cactus is one of the best sources for cactus water. Cut off its top, and crush the insides into a cup. Or cut off a piece of the insides and chew it. The water may be milky-looking, but it can keep you alive.

Sometimes you can find water holes in the desert; even muddy or scummy water tastes okay when you're thirsty. But if there are animal bones or bodies lying near the edge of the water hole, don't drink from it. The water could be

poisonous. You can harvest good water in the form of dew
drops from airplane wings or car hoods. Do this early in the
morning. Wipe the metal surfaces with a piece of cloth
then wring the water from the cloth into a container or suck
the water from the cloth. Some desert animals—the desert
tortoise, for instance—store water in their bodies. If you can
find them and eat them, your body can use the moisture in
their bodies.

Other animals make good food when you're hungry
enough. You can roast rattlesnakes or lizards, for instance.
A young cactus or a prickly pear also satisfies hunger. Scrape
off the thorns and stickers with a knife, a piece of glass, or
a rock before eating.

The more plants you see, the more chance you can find
something to eat. Not all plants are safe, however. If you're
not sure whether a plant is poisonous, don't eat much of it
at first. Pluck off a piece about the size of a pea. If water is
plentiful, boil the piece for a few minutes. Boiling can remove some poisons. Then touch the small piece to your
tongue. Does it taste sharply bitter? Does it make your
tongue numb? If so, throw it away. If it tastes all right, eat
the small piece and wait as long as possible to see how your
stomach reacts. If you still feel well after a day, go back to
the plant and eat a little bit more. Take it easy, and try to
vary your diet.

Forest and Jungle

Forests and jungles are rich in foods you probably hope
you'll never have to eat. Tree bark, for instance. In times of

famine, people have made bread from crushed bark. In an emergency, you can eat bark raw or cooked. Birch and willow barks have often been used to make a meal.

See any rotten logs? Dig into them with a stick and you may find grubs—rubbery, glistening wormlike animals. They can be eaten raw, although they're better when fried or boiled. Alligators are edible—if you can catch one. So are cooked grasshoppers. Some people think ants, termites, and frogs are delicious. Even if you don't, these animals can help drive away hunger.

It's often easier to find shelter and water in forests and jungles than it is in the desert. You can make a temporary home under a tree branch, or pile sticks against a tree to make a slanted roof. Rain water is safe to drink. So is muddy swamp water, even when it's smelly, provided you boil the water for at least three minutes before drinking it.

Snow-Covered Mountains

Water's no problem here. Clean melted snow is safe to drink, but don't take it cold. Let it melt in a cup or, better yet, heat it until it steams over a fire.

Snow can also provide a good shelter. Find a level spot if possible. Dig a hollow space big enough for you to disappear beneath the surface. If you scoop out the hollow beneath a low-lying tree branch, you'll have a ready-made roof; pile other cut branches on top.

If you have materials to make a fire, scoop out an extra space in the snow so you and the fire are in the same hollow. Leave the roof open above the fire so smoke can escape. Make a wall of logs, if you can, behind the fire so heat will be reflected toward you.

Build your fire slowly, starting with small scraps of bark or twigs. Add larger pieces carefully, and big logs last.

Start to build your shelter several hours before nightfall; that will give you time to do it right. If there are enough tree branches, make yourself a bed of boughs to keep your body raised several inches off the ground. Without the bed of branches, the ground will drain away your body's warmth. That can be uncomfortable, and dangerous.

One of the dangers is called hypothermia—a sudden major drop in body temperature. It strikes when your body is no longer able to keep itself heated. You're particularly prey to hypothermia when you're cold and tired. The first symptom is violent shivering. After that, hypothermia victims often don't know what's happening to them. Another symptom is slurred speech. Muscles tighten. Sometimes, the skin gets blue. In later stages, the victim passes out.

If you're with someone who begins showing these symptoms, move fast. People have been known to die from hypothermia within two hours. But quick action can prevent death. What should you do? Warm the victim up however you can.

One young woman out on a winter camping trip began shivering one night as she sat with friends near the entrance of a chilly cave. Within a few minutes, she had begun to talk nonsense. The two women with her wasted no time. They opened their jackets and held her close to share the warmth of their bodies. They also heated water over the fire in the cave and forced the woman to drink, to warm her inside. And they kept the woman talking and sitting up, even though she just wanted to go to sleep. In a short time, the symptoms began to disappear. The woman's body recovered its ability to warm itself up. Her friends—because they knew about hypothermia—had saved her life.

The amount of natural food on a mountain depends on how high you are. The Andes survivors (chapter 7) were driven to cannibalism because no edible plants grew, no animals lived where they had crashed. Down closer to sea level, mountains are sometimes stocked with food. Some pine trees, called piñons, for instance, bear edible, nutlike seeds. It's easy to track small game in the snow, to find rabbit or squirrel trails. All birds are edible, too.

Shelter, water, food—those are basic physical needs you can help meet while waiting for rescuers to arrive. There's more to survival, however, than conquering hunger, thirst, or exposure. There's also the challenge of conquering fear. What do you do, for instance, about the rustling noises in the darkness just outside the circle of light from your fire? What about the golden eyes you see glowing in the dark out there, looking at you and your little camp?

Sometimes such sights and sounds warn of danger. Often, they don't. Those frightening eyes, for instance, could belong to a curious bird or even a large but harmless insect. Your fear is natural, but try not to let it burden you or weigh down your hopes.

Keep your fire alight all night, with new wood. Keep your thoughts on home—the way Viktor Frankl did, and the

Apollo crew in dark space, and Roberto Canessa as he lay in his broken plane and thought of his mother.

You can never tell. Maybe you'll see your family in the morning.

Postscript

These true stories came from books, newspapers, magazine reports and personal interviews. I'm grateful for all the source material, and owe special thanks to historian James Axtell for his articles on Native Americans; Robert Nymeyer, a photographer in Carlsbad, N.M., for adding to research on Oliver Loving; and Air Force Master Sergeant David Eckelberg, a survival instructor at Fairchild Air Force Base in Washington, for advice on how to live through a disaster.

I'm thankful for several good books, some recent, some out of print, for supplying reliable data for my retelling. Among them:

Man's Search for Meaning by Viktor E. Frankl (Washington Square Press, 1963) tells his own concentration camp story and sketches his theory of psychiatric therapy. *Charles Goodnight, Cowman and Plainsman* by J. Evetts Haley, University of Oklahoma Press, 1949, gave the most complete picture of Oliver Loving's stand. Quinton Stockwell's own account of his ordeal appears in a book called *Indian Captivities or Life in the Wigwam,* edited by Samuel Gardner Drake and published in 1857 (Miller, Orton & Co.). John D. Morris described the search for Noah's Ark in a book called *Adventure on Ararat,* Creation Life Publishers, San Diego, 1973. The complete narrative of the Apollo 13 mission appeared in *13: The Flight that Failed* by Henry Cooper, Dial Press, 1973. Hiroo Onoda recalled many incidents of his thirty-year war in *No Surrender,* Dell Publishing Co., 1976; translation by Charles S. Terry. Two books told the story of the Springhill mine disaster: *Miracle at Springhill* by Leonard Lerner, Holt, Rinehart and Winston, N.Y., 1960; and *Individual and Group Behavior in a Coal Mine Disaster,* edited by H. D. Beach and R. A. Lucas, National Academy of Sciences, National Research Council, Publication 834, Washington, D.C., 1960. And Piers Paul Read was author of the authoritative book on the Andes plane crash survivors; it's called *Alive,* published in 1974 by J. B. Lippincott Co., Philadelphia and New York.

Index